First published in 2013. © Like Books & Design Ltd 2013
PRINTED IN CHINA

Whether you are creating a delicious cake, yummy cookies, flavoursome bread, a scrumptious dessert or pies with melt-in-your-mouth pastry there is nothing that lifts the heart like the smell of home baking filling your kitchen. This journal allows you to keep track of all your favourite baking recipes - whether they are your own tried and tested favourites, a recipe from a favourite restaurant, or a recipe lovingly passed down through your family and friends - there is plenty of space to include the recipes in the sections within the journal, or in the storage pocket at the back of the book.

Included are more than 50 easy to follow step-by-step recipes to help you on your way to creating your own definitive baking companion, which can be referred to time and again.

In baking there are many terms used in recipes for different cooking or mixing methods, and if you are not familiar with these terms a recipe can seem daunting, so here are some of the main terms you may come across when baking and an explanation of what they mean to help you with your baking techniques.

Boil   To cook until liquid is so hot it forms bubbles.

Broil   To cook directly under a heating element.

Chill   To place in the refrigerator to lower a food's temperature.

Chop   To cut into pieces with a sharp knife or chopper.

Combine   To mix ingredients together.

Cream   To beat until smooth, soft and fluffy.

Cube   To cut into 1/4inch cubes.

Cut   To mix a solid fat into a flour mixture with a pastry blender, a fork or two knives

Dice   To cut food into 1/8inch cubes.

Dot	Drop bits of butter or cheese here and there over food.
Drain	To pour off liquid.
Flour	To coat greased pans or dishes with a fine coat of flour. Shake out extra flour.
Fold	To mix gently by bringing rubber scraper down through mixture, across the bottom, up and over top until blended.
Fry	To cook in hot fat.
Garnish	To decorate a finished dish with colourful food to make it look pretty.
Grate	Rub against a grater to cut into small shreds.
Grease	To spread the bottom and/or sides of a pan with shortening to prevent sticking.
Grill	To cook directly over a heating element or hot coals.
Knead	To fold, turn, and press dough with heel of your hand in order to develop the gluten and make dough more elastic.
Ladle	To dip and serve liquid with a ladle.
Melt	To heat until it liquefies.
Mince	To chop or cut into tiny pieces.
Mix	To stir foods together.
Panfry	To cook in fat in a skillet.
Pare	To cut off the outside skin, as from an apple or potato.

Peel	To pull off the outer skin, as from a banana or an orange.
Pit	To take out the seeds.
Roll	Flatten and spread with a rolling pin.
Rubbing in	Rubbing pieces of cold diced butter or fat into flour using the fingertips and lifting the flour at the same time to avoid clumping.
Saute	To cook in small amount of fat in a skillet/frying pan.
Scald	To heat milk just below a boiling point. Tiny bubbles will form around the edge.
Shred	To cut into very thin strips.
Shortening	Modern shortening is a vegetable-based product, such as Crisco®, that is just barely solid at room temperature. Shortening has a higher smoke point than butter and margarine, leading to its use in deep-fat frying and as a pan coating to prevent baked goods from sticking.
Sift	To put dry ingredients like flour through a sifter or sieve.
Simmer	To cook in liquid over low heat so bubbles form slowly.
Stir	To mix round and round with a spoon.
Toss	To mix lightly.
Well	A hole made in dry ingredients in which you pour liquid.
Whip	To beat with a rotary egg beater or electric mixer to add air.

Happy baking!

bread recipes

Basic Bread Dough

Nothing is more satisfying than making your own bread.

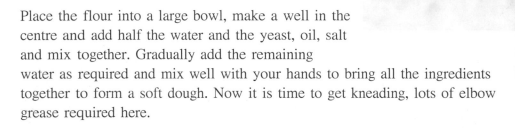

1kg/2.2lb strong bread flour
up to 625ml/just over 1 pint of tepid water
2 x 7g dried sachets of yeast
1 tbsp salt
1 tbsp vegetable oil

Place the flour into a large bowl, make a well in the
centre and add half the water and the yeast, oil, salt
and mix together. Gradually add the remaining
water as required and mix well with your hands to bring all the ingredients
together to form a soft dough. Now it is time to get kneading, lots of elbow
grease required here.

Place the dough on a lightly floured work surface, then using the heel of your
hand, push the dough back and forth, you can be quite aggressive doing this,
you are trying to work the gluten in the flour as this will create a silky
smooth elastic dough. Continue to knead the dough for 5-10 minutes.

The next step is to leave the dough to prove (proving is allowing the dough to
rise, just sit back and watch the yeast work its magic). Place the dough back
into the bowl and cover with a clean tea towel or a sheet of lightly oiled
clingfilm and place in a warm draught free place for 45 minutes or until the
dough has doubled in size. Proving the bread improves the flavour and the
texture of the bread.

Once the dough has doubled in size it is time to knock the air out of it (this
is referred to as knocking back). The purpose of this process is to distribute
the fermented yeast in the dough. Simply bash and squash the dough for 30
seconds.

Shape the bread and give it a second proving. This is the most important part,
as the second prove will give you the air that ends up in the bread, giving you
a light soft texture.

It is time to decide what shape you want your finished loaf or rolls or pizza bases to be. Go ahead be creative, try making a plait or long French stick. Simply place into bread tins or create your own shapes, which ever you choose you must allow the dough to prove for a second time. Cover as before, leave in a warm place until once again the dough has doubled in size, this will take about 45 minutes to an hour.

Bake the bread in a preheated oven at 200C/400F/Gas mark 6, a loaf will take approximately 35-45 minutes and smaller rolls will take about 20-25 minutes to cook. To test the bread, tap the bottom of the loaf with your finger and if it sounds hollow then your bread is cooked. Remove from the oven, leave to cool and use as required.

Soda Bread (Makes 1 loaf)

Soda bread is the easiest bread to make as it requires very little kneading and no waiting for the dough to rise.

375g/13oz plain flour, plus extra for dusting
150g/5oz wholemeal flour
1 tsp salt
1 tsp bicarbonate of soda
50g/2oz butter, melted
1 tbsp black treacle
300-340ml/11-12 fl oz buttermilk, or warm milk
mixed with 1 tbsp lemon juice

Method

Preheat the oven to 200C/400F/Gas mark 6. Place the flour, salt and bicarbonate of soda into a large mixing bowl and mix together. Make a large well in the centre and pour in the melted butter and treacle (the treacle will give the loaf an earthy taste, darken the crumb and help crisp up the crust), plus enough buttermilk to form a loose sticky dough.

Tip the dough onto a lightly floured works surface. The dough will be quite sticky. Briefly knead the dough for one minute, then shape the dough into a large ball. Place the dough onto a baking tray and flatten the top slightly.

Take a wooden spoon and dust the handle with some extra flour, then hold it horizontally over the dough and press down with the handle through the dough until you almost reach the baking tray. This mark is the trademark soda bread cross. Repeat with a line at right angles to this to create a cross in the top making 4 quarters.

Dust the dough with flour and bake in the preheated oven for 30-40 minutes, or until the bread is deep golden brown, has risen nicely and the dough inside where you made the cross is not damp. Remove from the oven, leave to cool slightly and serve. This bread does not keep well, so it's best eaten on the day you make it, however any left over can be used for toast.

Walnut & Honey Bread

(Makes 2 loaves)

500g/1lb 2oz wholemeal flour
4 tsps baking powder
good pinch of salt
200g/7oz walnuts
200g/7oz honey
280ml/10 fl oz water

Method

Preheat the oven to 200C/400F/Gas mark 6. Place the honey in a small pan over a low heat just to soften the honey slightly. Blend half the walnuts in a food processor or place them in a clean tea towel and bash with a rolling pin until the nuts are almost powder like in texture. Crush the remaining nuts very coarsely.

Mix together the nuts, flour and baking powder into a bowl. Add the honey and water and mix thoroughly together until well combined. Knead very briefly to form a stiff dough. Divide the dough into two and shape into rough round shapes.

Flatten out the dough with the palm of your hand about 5cm high, then using the handle of a wooden spoon, lightly dusted with flour, create a cross in the bread, pushing the handle down almost to the base.

Bake the loaves in the preheated oven for 20-25 minutes, or until the bread sounds hollow when tapped at the base. Remove from the oven and allow to cool slightly on a wire rack.

Brioche (Makes 2 small loaves)

A classic French bread, rich in butter and slightly sweet with a soft golden crust and a delightful yellow buttery texture. It is widely eaten in France, with coffee for breakfast, as a roll with dinner, or as a base for any number of desserts.

400g/14oz strong white bread flour
110g/4oz butter, softened
1 x 7g sachet, dried yeast
good pinch of salt
85ml/3 fl oz warm milk
2 tbsps caster sugar
4 eggs, beaten
For the glaze
1 egg
2 tbsps milk

Method

In a large bowl, simply combine all the ingredients together to form a dough. Knead the dough on a lightly floured works surface for about 10 minutes until smooth and silky. Shape the dough into a round, place in a bowl, cover tightly and leave in the fridge overnight.

Divide the dough into two and form into two loaves, the shape of your choice. Lightly dust the loaves with flour, place onto a lightly floured baking tray and cover with a loose fitting bag or clean tea towel. Set aside to prove in a warm place until the loaves have doubled in size, this could take up to 4 hours as the dough is cold.

Preheat the oven to 200C/400F/Gas mark 6. To make the glaze, simply beat the egg and milk together. Brush the loaves all over with the glaze.

Bake in the oven for 10 minutes, then lower the oven temperature to 180C/350F/Gas mark 4 and continue baking for a further 30 minutes, or until golden brown. Remove from the oven and allow the loaves to cool on a wire rack.

Focaccia Bread (Makes 1 loaf)

Impress your friends with this easy Italian bread recipe, which is delicious and far better than anything shop bought.

500g/1lb 2oz strong white bread flour
1 x 7g sachet dried yeast
2 tsps salt
up to 150-200ml/7 fl oz warm water
85ml/3 fl oz olive oil
For the topping
sprigs fresh rosemary
olive oil
coarse sea salt

Method

Combine the flour, yeast, olive oil, and salt in a mixer with a dough hook. (This stage can easily be done by hand, but far easier using a mixer, but not as satisfying). Add enough water to make a soft dough, and knead in the mixer or by hand for about 5 minutes until the dough is smooth and shiny.

Transfer the dough to an oiled bowl, cover with a tea towel and leave in a warm place for about 45 minutes until well risen. Tip the dough out onto a floured surface and knead to knock out any air pockets. Roll the dough out into an oval like shape about 2cm thick. Transfer to an oiled baking tray. Firmly press your finger tips into the bread dough to form little pockets.

For the topping, place a really good drizzle of olive oil into a small bowl or pestle and mortar, add a generous handful of small sprigs of fresh rosemary, then thoroughly mix with the oil to create a fragrant infused oil.

Pour the flavoured oil on top of the bread dough, then using your fingertips, press the oil into all the small pockets over the dough until the dough is evenly covered with the oil. Sprinkle over some coarse sea salt. Cover the bread with a tea towel and set the loaf aside for another 20 minutes.

Meanwhile preheat the oven to 200C/400F/Gas mark 6. Transfer the loaf to the centre shelf of the oven and cook for about 15 minutes until well risen and golden brown. Remove from the oven, this bread is best served straight from the oven.

Optional: Try flavouring your bread with garlic, olives, chilli, fresh basil, grated fresh parmesan cheese, tomatoes, grilled peppers, just let your imagination run away with you.

Olive & Fennel Loaf (Makes 1 loaf)

700g/1 1/2lb strong white bread flour
1/2 tsp salt
1 tsp sugar
1 x 7g sachet dried yeast
2 tsps fennel seeds, toasted and roughly crushed
2 tsps olive oil
7 tbsps quartered Kalamata olives, drained
425ml/15 fl oz warm water

Method

Sift the flour and salt into a large bowl and stir in the sugar and yeast with half the fennel seeds, 1 tbsp of the oil and 425ml of lukewarm water. Mix to a soft dough, then transfer to a floured worksurface. Knead for 6-8 minutes, until smooth and elastic.

Knead in the olives until evenly distributed. Place in a clean, oiled bowl and cover with a clean tea towel. Set aside in a warm place for 1-2 hours, until doubled in size.

Turn the dough out onto the worksurface and knead again briefly. Shape into a sausage shape about 32cm long and slash the top a few times with a sharp knife. Transfer to a lightly oiled baking sheet. Scatter the rest of the fennel seeds and a little flaked sea salt over the top. Drizzle over the rest of the oil. Cover with a tea towel and leave to rise again for 20 minutes.

Preheat the oven to 230C/450F/Gas mark 8. Bake the loaf for 30-35 minutes, until risen and golden, and hollow sounding when tapped on the base. Cool on a wire rack.

15

Spiced Moroccan Flatbreads (Makes 4)

150g/5oz plain flour
150g/5oz wholemeal flour
1 x 7g sachet dried yeast
1 tbsp melted butter
110ml/4 fl oz tepid water
2 cloves garlic, peeled
2 tsps sesame seeds
1/2 red chilli, de-seeded
2 tsps ground fenugreek seeds or ground coriander
2 tbsps olive oil
2 tbsps chopped fresh coriander

Method

Use a food processor or pestle and mortar to blend the garlic, chilli, fresh coriander, oil, sesame seeds and ground spice to a thick paste. In a large bowl, add the flours, yeast and a teaspoon of salt and combine together. Stir in the water into the melted butter, then mix this into the flour, adding a little extra water if required, to form a smooth dough. Mix in the spiced paste until fully incorporated into the dough.

Knead the dough on a lightly floured surface for 5 minutes, then return to the bowl, cover and leave in a warm place until the dough has doubled in size, this should take about an hour. Knock back the dough and knead lightly, then divide into 8 balls, then roll out on the floured surface to a rough 18cm circle about the thickness of a 10p coin. Prick each one well with a fork to stop them rising. Place a heavy based frying pan over a medium high heat.

Place the flatbreads in the dry frying pan and cook for 1-2 minutes on either side, until the breads are lightly charred and golden. (Alternatively, the breads can be cooked under a grill set to the highest setting.) Keep the bread warm and continue to cook the bread in batches.

Newcastle Brown Ale® & Cheese Loaf

(Makes 1 loaf)

300g/10 1/2oz strong white bread flour
150g/5oz wholemeal flour
1 tsp yeast
4 tsps sugar
1 tsp salt
1 egg, beaten
225ml/8 fl oz Newcastle Brown Ale®, warmed to tepid
25g/1oz powdered milk
110g/4oz cheddar cheese, grated
50g/2oz parmesan cheese, grated
1 tsp fennel seeds
1 tsp English mustard powder

Method

Dissolve the sugar and yeast in the warmed beer and leave to stand for 5 minutes. In a large mixing bowl, mix the flour, cheese, salt, fennel seeds, mustard powder, milk powder and the egg until well combined. Stir in the yeast, ale and sugar mixture to form a soft dough.

Turn the dough out onto a lightly floured surface and knead for 10-15 minutes until the dough is smooth and elastic. Form the dough into a large cob shape and place onto a baking sheet. Lightly cover with oiled cling film and allow to prove in a warm place until the dough has doubled in size.

Meanwhile preheat the oven to 200C/400F/Gas mark 6. When the dough has doubled in size cut a cross in the top of the dough and bake in the preheated oven for 25-30 minutes until well risen and the base of the loaf sounds hollow when lightly tapped. Remove from the oven, allow to cool and serve.

Bagels (Makes 12)

The cooking of bagels is really something quite unique as the dough is poached in water before you bake them, and it's this pre-poaching that gives the bagel it's distinctive texture and characteristics, where the centre should be almost chewy.

500g/1lb 2oz strong white bread flour
1 x 7g sachet, dried yeast
good pinch of salt
250ml/9 fl oz warm water
25g/1oz caster sugar
50ml/2 fl oz vegetable oil
To finish
1 egg, beaten
poppy or sesame seeds (optional)

Method

To make the bagel dough, simply combine all the ingredients in a large bowl to form a dough. Transfer the dough onto a lightly floured work surface and knead for about 10 minutes until smooth, shiny and elastic in texture.

Shape the dough into a round, lightly rub with a little extra oil and place into a clean bowl. Cover the dough with a loose fitting bag or a sheet of clingfilm and set aside to prove until doubled in size.

When the dough has doubled in size, knock it back to deflate it and divide into 12 equal pieces. Using your hands, roll out the dough into sausage shapes about 15cm long. Wet the ends of the dough with water, pressing the ends together and form into rings. Place the dough rings onto a lightly oiled baking sheet, cover them lightly and set aside, somewhere warm to prove until doubled in size.

Preheat the oven to 200C/400F/Gas mark 6. In a large shallow pan bring some water up to the boil. When the dough has doubled in size, then they are ready for poaching. You will have to poach the bagels in batches to avoid overcrowding the pan.

Reduce the water to a simmer, then carefully slip the bagels into the water and poach for one minute on either side and allow them to puff up. Remove the bagels from the water with a perforated spoon and allow to drain on a clean tea towel.

You may find that some of the bagels have come unstuck and un-rolled during the poaching, but don't worry you can simply stick the ends back together. Lay the Bagels onto lightly oiled baking trays, brush over the beaten egg to glaze and sprinkle with the poppy or sesame seeds if desired.

Bake in the preheated oven for 15 minutes, or until the bagels are beautifully glossy and golden brown. Remove from the oven and allow to cool on a wire rack.

My recipes

Recipe	Thick Pancakes
Serves	12 pancakes
Preparation time	15 Minutes
Notes/tips	Do not allow mixture to become too thin or the pancakes will not be thick.

* Blueberries / Chocolate Chips can be added

Ingredients	Amount
Self-Raising Soda Bread Flour	8oz
Caster Sugar	3oz
Eggs	1 egg
Butter Milk	500ml (approx.)

Method

Sieve the flour and sugar into a large bowl. Make a well in centre of the bowl and add the whisked egg. Mix together and then add, bit by bit, the butter milk. Once the batter feels thick spoon onto griddle. Once bubbles appear on surface of pancake, flip. Place on a moist teatowl and serve with sugar, butter, jam, lemon juice or chocolate spread.

My recipes

Recipe ---

Serves ---

Preparation time ---

Notes/tips ---

Ingredients

--- ---

--- ---

--- ---

--- ---

--- ---

--- ---

--- ---

--- ---

Method

My recipes

Recipe ....

Serves ....

Preparation time ....

Notes/tips ....

....

....

....

Ingredients

....

....

....

....

....

....

....

....

....

Method

My recipes

Recipe   ---

Serves   ---

Preparation time   ---

Notes/tips

Ingredients

-------------------------------   -------------------------------

-------------------------------   -------------------------------

-------------------------------   -------------------------------

-------------------------------   -------------------------------

-------------------------------   -------------------------------

-------------------------------   -------------------------------

-------------------------------   -------------------------------

-------------------------------   -------------------------------

Method

My recipes

Recipe --

Serves --

Preparation time --

Notes/tips --

Ingredients

--   --

--   --

--   --

--   --

--   --

--   --

--   --

--   --

Method

My recipes

Recipe --

Serves --

Preparation time --

Notes/tips --

Ingredients

--   --

--   --

--   --

--   --

--   --

--   --

--   --

--   --

Method

My recipes

Recipe ....

Serves ....

Preparation time ....

Notes/tips ....

....

....

....

Ingredients ....

....

....

....

....

....

....

....

Method

cake recipes

Victoria Sponge

(Cuts into 12 slices)

4 medium sized eggs room temperature
225g/8oz caster sugar, plus a little
extra for sprinkling to finish
225g/8oz self raising flour
1 tsp baking powder
225g/8oz soft butter,
plus a little extra to grease the tins
jam of your choice to fill the cake
lightly whipped cream (optional)

Method

Preheat the oven to 180C/350F/Gas
mark 4. Grease and line two
20cm/8inch sandwich tins with baking
parchment. Rub a little butter around
the base and sides of the tin and line
the base with a disc of parchment
paper, to do this draw a circle onto the
paper around the tin and cut out.

In a large bowl cream together the
butter and sugar until pale light and
fluffy, this can be done in a food
mixer, using a hand held electric whisk
or by hand using a wooden spoon.
Sieve the flour and baking powder into
a large bowl. Crack the eggs into a
small bowl and gently whisk together
using a fork. Gradually add the beaten
eggs to the creamed butter and sugar
mixture, a little at a time continuously
beating as you add the eggs.

If the mixture starts to curdle, don't worry, simply add a little flour to the mixture and continue to beat. Gradually add the remaining eggs, then fold in the sifted flour until well combined.

Do not overwork the mix, as soon as everything is well blended you should stop. The finished mixture should be of a soft dropping consistency - it should easily fall off a spoon. If the mixture feels a little stiff, gradually beat in a tbsp of milk until the mixture is the correct consistency.

Divide the mixture evenly between the two lined sandwich tins, use a spatula to gently smooth the surface of the cakes. Place the tins on the middle shelf of the preheated oven and bake for 20-25 minutes or until the cakes are well risen, lightly golden brown and when lightly pressed with your finger should spring back to the touch. Remove the tins from the oven and leave to cool in the tins for 5 minutes.

Run a palette or rounded butter knife around the edges of the tin and carefully turn out onto a wire cooling rack. To avoid leaving wire marks on the cake, simply place a clean tea towel over the tin, put your hand on the tea towel and turn the tin upside down, the cake will come out onto your hand and tea towel, then you can turn it over from your hand onto the wire rack. Set the cake aside to cool completely.

To finish the cake, place one cake upside down on a plate or cake stand and spread with plenty of jam, top with the second cake, top side up and gently sandwich together. If you overfill the cake with jam it will ooze down the sides of the cake but I think this looks really appealing. If you are looking for a more professional and neat finish do not over fill the sponge with jam, simply leave a slight border around the edge, the jam will spread to the edge as you sandwich the two cakes together. If you want, you can fill the cake with some lightly whipped cream. To finish, dust the top of the cake with a sprinkling of caster sugar or icing sugar. Cut into slices and serve.

Madeira Cake (Serves 10)

A classic tea time treat, this recipe has a zingy lemon icing, but the cake is also delicious simply served un-iced, with the addition of some candied lemon peel sprinkled over the top.

200g/7oz plain flour
1 tsp baking powder
150g/5oz butter
150g/5oz caster sugar
4 eggs
2 lemons, grated zest and 2 tbsps lemon juice
For the topping
150g/5oz icing sugar
1 1/2 tbsp lemon juice

Method

Preheat the oven to 180C/350F/Gas mark 4. Lightly grease and line a 20x10cm loaf tin with baking parchment. Sieve together the flour and baking powder.

In a large bowl, beat together the butter, sugar and lemon zest until light, fluffy and creamy in texture. Add the eggs one at a time, adding a tablespoon of flour between each egg. Beat the mixture thoroughly before adding the next egg. Fold in the remaining flour with a large metal spoon and fold in the lemon juice.

Spoon the mixture into the prepared loaf tin and spread out lightly and evenly with the back of a spoon. Bake in the preheated oven for about 50 minutes, or until the cake is well risen, springy to the touch and a skewer inserted in the centre comes out clean. Remove from the oven, leave to cool in the tin for 10 minutes, then turn out to cool on a wire rack.

Meanwhile, to make the topping, sift the icing sugar into a large bowl. Beat in the lemon juice, a little at a time, until the icing is smooth and glossy and fairly stiff. Spread the icing over the cooled cake, cut into slices and serve.

Battenberg

Layers of coloured sponge, creating a checker board effect, encased in marzipan, make this cake a really impressive and simply delicious classic tea time treat.

175g/6oz butter, softened
175g/6oz caster sugar
3 eggs
175g/6oz self raising flour
1/2 tsp vanilla extract
red food colouring
To cover the cake
450g/1lb marzipan
4 tbsps apricot jam
icing sugar for dusting

Method

Preheat the oven to 190C/375F/Gas mark 5. Grease a 20cm/8inch square, loose bottomed cake tin with a little butter and line with parchment paper.

Take a 30 x 20cm/12 x 8inch strip of parchment paper and make a 8cm/3inch fold in the centre. This folded paper will create a division in the cake tin, so that the two differently coloured sponges can be cooked at the same time. Place the folded paper neatly inside the tin.

Cream together the butter and sugar in a large bowl until light and fluffy. Add the eggs one at a time, adding a sieved tablespoon of flour in between each addition, beating thoroughly to create a smooth mixture. Beat in the remaining flour and stir in the vanilla extract. Divide the cake mixture between 2 bowls, adding a touch of red food colouring to half the cake mixture and mix well until thoroughly blended. Spoon the two cake mixtures into the two divided sections of the baking tin.

Bake in the preheated oven for about 25 minutes, or until well risen, springy to the touch and a skewer inserted in the centre comes out clean. Remove from the oven and leave to cool in the tin for 10 minutes. Slide a knife around the edge of each sponge and turn out onto wire rack to cool.

To assemble the cake, place one sponge on top of the other and trim of the edges to create a neat finish, making sure both sponges are of identical size. Cut the sponges in half lengthways to create four long rectangles.

Warm the apricot jam in a small pan and push through a fine sieve, the jam will be used to create the glue to stick the sponges together.

Brush the long side of one of the sponges with the jam and sandwich it together with a sponge of a contrasting colour. Repeat the process with the remaining two strips of sponge. Sandwich the two pairs of sponge together to form a checker board effect. then brush the sides and top with the apricot jam.

Roll out the marzipan on a clean works surface lightly dusted with icing sugar to a size of appropriately 40 x 20cm/16 x 10inch, it should be large enough to completely cover the cake, but leaving the ends exposed.

Turn the sponge upside down onto the marzipan and brush the underside of the sponge with jam. Carefully wrap the marzipan around the sponges and lightly press the join together to form a neat seam. Turn the cake over so that the seam is underneath on the bottom of the cake. Using a sharp knife, trim away any excess marzipan to create a neat finish. Cut the cake into slices and serve.

Stem Ginger & Chocolate Chunk Cake

Such a delicious easy cake to prepare, as all the ingredients are prepared in a single saucepan. Soft moist ginger cake with chunky chocolate treats running through the centre.

50g/2oz muscovado sugar
2 tbsps black treacle
75g/2 1/2oz honey
110g/4oz butter, diced
100ml/3 1/2 fl oz milk
75g/2 1/2oz chopped stem ginger in syrup
1 large egg, beaten
225g/8oz plain flour
1/4 tsp salt
1 tsp bicarbonate of soda
1 x 100g/3 1/2oz bar chocolate

Method

Heat the oven to 180C/350F/Gas mark 4. Place the sugar, black treacle, honey, butter, milk and chopped ginger into a saucepan large enough to hold all the ingredients, place over a low heat, stir occasionally until gently melted.

Remove the pan from the heat, leave to cool for a few minutes then stir in the beaten egg. Sieve the flour, salt and bicarbonate of soda into the pan and mix well until thoroughly combined. Break up the chocolate bar into small bite sized pieces and stir into the mixture. Spoon the mixture into a 450g/1lb loaf tin and spread evenly.

Bake in the oven for 40-45 minutes or until a skewer inserted in the centre comes out clean. Remove from the oven and place the tin on a cooling rack to cool completely before turning out. Store in an airtight container.

Banana & Hazelnut Cake (Serves 6-8)

280g/10oz self raising flour
1 tsp baking powder
1 x 284ml pot soured cream
1 tsp vanilla extract
100g/3 1/2oz unsalted butter, melted
150g/5oz caster sugar
2 large eggs
For the topping
100g/3 1/2oz plain flour
100g/3 1/2oz hazelnuts, finely chopped
120g/4 1/2oz light brown muscovado sugar
1/2 tsp salt
3 large bananas
juice of 1 lemon
100g/3 1/2oz unsalted butter, melted

Method

Preheat the oven to 180C/350F/Gas mark 4. Grease a 25cm square cake tin and line with baking parchment.

To make the topping, place the flour in a large bowl with the hazelnuts, sugar and salt. Pour over the melted butter, then mix with a round-bladed knife until it resembles rough crumbs. Chill until needed.

To make the cake, place all the ingredients in a large bowl and beat together until the mixture is smooth and thoroughly combined. Spoon into the tin and smooth with the back of a spoon.

Peel and slice the bananas, then toss with lemon juice in a bowl. Scatter the bananas evenly over the surface of the cake mixture, then sprinkle over the hazelnut topping.

Bake for 45-50 minutes, until a skewer inserted into the centre comes out clean. Cool for 10 minutes in the tin, then lift out. Serve warm or cold.

Carrot Cake (Serves 8-10)

2 eggs
110g/4oz dark brown soft sugar
75ml/2 1/2 fl oz sunflower oil
175g/6oz carrots, grated (about 2 medium carrots)
50g/2oz desiccated coconut
50g/2oz sultanas
110g/4oz self-raising flour
1 tsp ground cinnamon
1/2 tsp ground nutmeg
For the topping
110g/4oz cream cheese
225g/8oz icing sugar
1 orange, zest
handful of halved walnuts (optional)

Method

Preheat the oven to 180C/350F/Gas mark 4. Grease an 18cm square tin and line the base with greaseproof paper. Whisk together the eggs and sugar, then slowly whisk in the oil. Stir in the remaining cake ingredients, combining well.

Turn the mixture into the tin, place on a baking sheet and bake for 25 - 30 minutes. Test the cake to see if it is cooked - insert a skewer and this should come out with a few moist crumbs on it. Remove from the tin and cool on a wire rack.

For the icing, beat together the cream cheese, icing sugar and orange zest and spread over the cake. If you prefer, you can make double the topping mixture, slice the cake in half and use half of the topping to sandwich together the sliced pieces - then top with remaining icing. Add walnuts if using.

Decadent Chocolate Raspberry Cake

(Serves 6-8)

300g/10 1/2oz dark chocolate
225g/8oz unsalted butter
5 medium eggs
75g/2 1/2oz golden caster sugar
75g/2 1/2oz plain flour
1 tsp ground cinnamon
250g/9oz fresh raspberries
icing sugar, for dusting

Method

Preheat the oven to 170C/325F/Gas mark 3. Grease and base line a round 23cm cake tin. Place 250g of the chocolate and the butter in a bowl set over a pan of simmering water, making sure the base of the bowl does not touch the water. Heat, stirring occasionally, until melted. Stir and leave to cool slightly.

Using an electric whisk, beat together the eggs and sugar for 4-5 minutes until thick and pale. Very gently fold the melted chocolate mixture into the whisked eggs.

Sift the flour and cinnamon over the mixture and fold in. Pour into the prepared tin and sprinkle 175g/6oz raspberries evenly over the top, reserving the remaining raspberries for decoration.

Bake for 35-45 minutes, or until the cake is risen and firm to the touch. Cool in the tin for 15 minutes before turning out onto a plate. When cool, dust with sifted icing sugar.

When ready to serve, place the remaining chocolate and 2 tsps cold water in a pan and heat very gently until melted and smooth. Cool slightly. To serve, place a slice of cake on each plate and decorate with a little chocolate sauce and a few reserved raspberries. Best eaten on the same day as cooked.

Elderflower Cupcakes

(Makes 12)

175g/6oz unsalted butter, softened
175g/6oz caster sugar
3 eggs
5 tbsps elderflower cordial
175g/6oz self-raising flour
pinch of salt
For the icing
110g/4oz unsalted butter, softened
110g/4oz icing sugar
3 tbsps elderflower cordial
50g/2oz cream cheese
For the topping
white icing flowers, for decorating (optional)

Method

Preheat the oven to 180C/350F/Gas mark 4. Line a 12-hole muffin tin with paper cases. Using electric beaters, cream together the butter and sugar in a bowl for 5 - 6 minutes until pale and fluffy.

In a jug, gently whisk together the eggs and cordial. Add a spoonful of flour to the creamed butter then slowly pour in the egg mixture, beating constantly. Sift the remaining flour and a pinch of salt into the mixture and fold in until evenly combined.

Place heaped tablespoons of the batter into the cases and bake for 18 - 20 minutes until the cakes are golden and spring back when touched. Cool on a wire rack.

For the icing, cream the butter, icing sugar and cordial together for 3 - 4 minutes until light and fluffy. Beat in the cream cheese until you have a thick, creamy icing. Spread or pipe over the cupcakes and decorate with icing flowers, if using.

Recipe   Aunt Janets Chocolate Cake

Serves   Two round Sponges (Double Cake)

Preparation time   15 - 20 mins

Notes/tips   Remember to lower
temperature of oven when cake
is added in.

Ingredients

Cake

8oz margerine

10oz Caster Sugar

8oz self raising flour

8 desert spoons hot water

4 dtsp cocoa powder

4 eggs

Icing

6oz icing sugar

3oz butter (soft)

Method

Mix the cocoa with hot water and leave to cool. Cream the margerine and suger, beat in the eggs and 3/4 of the cocoa. Fold in the flour. Divide the mixtures evenly into two ~~smooth~~ Sandwich tins. Bake in a preheated oven for 27 minutes ~~in~~ at 180°C as soon as the cake is placed in the oven reduce the heat to 165°C.

To make icing beat the icing suger and butter together until smooth then add remaining cocoa. Spread evenly on cooled sponges.

My recipes

Recipe ___Peach Yogurt Cake___

Serves ___Double qunty makes 2 large tins + 1 small___

Preparation time ___15mins___

Notes/tips ___Grease and line the loaf___
___tins.___
___* Carton = yogurt carton.___

___

Ingredients

1 carton of peach yogurt
3 cartons self raising flour
2 cartons caster suger
1 carton cooking oil
3 eggs

Method

Beat all the ingredients together
for 3 minutes and divide evenly
into loaf tins. Bake for 40
minutes in a preheated oven
at 155°C.

My recipes

Recipe ___Brownies___

Serves ___24___

Preparation time ___½ hour___

Notes/tips ___Use Cadburys Chocolate___

✳ Line tray with tinfoil ✳

Ingredients

175g Margarine/butter

175g Chocolate

3 eggs

250g caster sugar

75g plain flour

40g cocoa powder

Method

Melt the butter and chocolate together over a pan of water. Mix together the eggs and sugar then stir in the melted butter and chocolate. Sieve in the flour and cocoa powder. Place in a lined tray for 30 mins in a preheated oven at 180°C.

My recipes

Recipe ---

Serves ---

Preparation time ---

Notes/tips ---

Ingredients ---

--- ---

--- ---

--- ---

--- ---

--- ---

--- ---

--- ---

--- ---

Method

My recipes

Recipe ---

Serves ---

Preparation time ---

Notes/tips ---

Ingredients

--- ---

--- ---

--- ---

--- ---

--- ---

--- ---

--- ---

--- ---

Method

My recipes

Recipe _____

Serves _____

Preparation time _____

Notes/tips _____

_____

_____

_____

Ingredients

_____ _____

_____ _____

_____ _____

_____ _____

_____ _____

_____ _____

_____ _____

_____ _____

Method

My recipes

Recipe   --

Serves   --

Preparation time   --

Notes/tips   --

Ingredients

------------------------------- --

------------------------------- --

------------------------------- --

------------------------------- --

------------------------------- --

------------------------------- --

------------------------------- --

------------------------------- --

Method

biscuit recipes

Big Chewy Chocolate Chip Cookies

(Makes 20)

250g/9oz plain flour
1/2 tsp bicarbonate of soda
1/2 tsp salt
175g/6oz unsalted butter (melted)
200g/7oz dark brown soft sugar
100g/3 1/2oz caster sugar
1 tbsp vanilla extract
1 egg
1 egg yolk
325g/11oz chocolate chips

Method

Preheat the oven to 170C/325F/Gas mark 3. Grease baking trays or line with parchment. Sift together the flour, bicarbonate of soda and salt; set aside.

In a medium bowl, cream together the melted butter, brown sugar and caster sugar until well blended. Beat in the vanilla, egg and egg yolk until light and creamy. Mix in the sifted ingredients until just blended. Stir in the chocolate chips by hand using a wooden spoon.

Drop cookie dough onto the prepared baking trays, with each cookie around 4 tablespoons of dough (for smaller cookies, drop 1 rounded tablespoon and adjust baking time as necessary). Do not flatten the dough. Cookies should be about 8cm apart.

Bake for 15 to 17 minutes in the preheated oven, or until the edges are lightly toasted. Cool on baking trays for a few minutes before transferring to wire racks to cool completely.

All-Butter Scottish Shortbread Cookies

(Makes 12)

This luxurious all-butter shortbread is simple but classic.

175g/6oz plain flour
110g/4oz caster sugar
175g/6oz butter

Method

Preheat oven to 150C/300F/Gas mark 2. Cream together the butter and sugar and fold in the flour to form a soft dough. Press into a 23cm (9inch) buttered baking dish. Prick top with a fork.

Bake until pale golden brown on the edges, approximately 30 to 40 minutes. Cool and cut into squares.

Pistachio & Chocolate Biscotti

(Serves 4)

Classic Italian biscuits, wonderful to serve with strong black coffee or to dunk into ice cold limoncello.

50g/2oz pistachio nuts, shelled
25g/1oz dark chocolate chips
110g/4oz plain flour
50g/2oz caster sugar
1 tsp baking powder
few drops vanilla extract
1 egg yolk

Method

Preheat the oven to 180C/350F/Gas mark 4. Sieve the flour and baking powder into a mixing bowl, stir in the sugar, chocolate chips and nuts. Add the egg yolk and mix well to create a dough.

Lightly knead the dough until smooth on a lightly floured surface, then shape the dough into a log shape and place on a baking sheet lined with baking parchment paper.

Bake in the preheated oven for 20 minutes, remove from the oven and allow to cool slightly. Slice the log diagonally into slices about 1cm thick.

Place the slices back onto the baking tray and return to the oven for 5-6 minutes to allow the biscuits to crisp up. Remove from the oven, allow to cool and serve.

Whoopie Pies (Makes 8)

Whoopie pies are two soft cookies sandwiched together with delicious filling. It is a cross between a soft biscuit, a cake and a pie.

200g/7oz light brown soft sugar
150g/5oz butter, softened
1 egg, beaten
350g/12oz plain flour
50g/2oz cocoa powder
1 tsp bicarbonate of soda
pinch of salt
250ml/9 fl oz buttermilk
For the filling
150g/5oz butter, softened
250g/9oz icing sugar
few drops vanilla extract
For the topping
150g/5oz icing sugar
2 tbsps cocoa powder

Method

Preheat the oven to 180C/350F/Gas mark 4. Line 2 baking trays with baking parchment. To make the pies, cream together the butter and sugar in a bowl until pale, light and fluffy. In a separate bowl, sieve together the flour, cocoa powder, salt and bicarbonate of soda. Gradually add spoonfuls of the flour mixture into the creamed butter and sugar along with the buttermilk, mixing well after each addition, to make a smooth, thick cake like mixture.

Using a 5cm diameter ice cream scoop, or tablespoon, drop 6-8 scoops of the mixture onto each baking tray, spacing them well apart to allow room to spread out during baking. Bake for 12-14 minutes or until well risen, lightly cracked and firm to the touch. Remove from the oven, leave to cool slightly on the trays, then remove to a wire rack to cool completely.

To make the filling, beat the butter in a bowl, then gradually add the sieved icing sugar, beating well to create a smooth spreadable icing. Add a few drops of vanilla extract and stir through. To make the topping, sieve together the icing sugar and cocoa powder into a bowl, then gradually add 4-6 teaspoons of warm water to make a smooth, glossy spreadable icing.

Carefully spread the topping over half the pies, smoothing the icing over with the back of a knife. Decorate the tops with chocolate sprinkles and set aside to set the icing. When the icing top has set, spoon or pipe the filling onto the flat sides of the remaining pies and carefully sandwich together.

Millionaires' Shortbread Cookies (Makes 10)

Crisp shortbread base, soft caramel centre topped with chocolate, simply delicious!

200g/7oz shortbread biscuits (crushed)
25g/1oz butter (melted)
For filling
150g/5oz butter
150g/5oz dark brown soft sugar
400g/14oz can condensed milk
For topping
200g/7oz milk or dark chocolate (melted)

Method

Line a 18cm (7inch) square tin with baking parchment. For the base, mix the crushed biscuits with the melted butter and then lightly press the mixture into the prepared tin to make an even layer. Chill for 20 minutes.

For the filling, place the butter and sugar into a non-stick pan and stir over a medium heat until the butter melts and the sugar dissolves. To make the caramel, add the condensed milk, stirring continuously, until the first bubbles appear on the surface. Remove from the heat as soon as it comes to the boil.

Spread the caramel evenly over the crumb base and then cool and chill for about half an hour. Pour the melted chocolate over the caramel, smoothing to the edges. When the chocolate has cooled and set, cut into squares.

Digestive Cookies (Makes 24)

150g/5oz plain wholemeal flour
1 tsp baking powder
1/2 tsp salt
1/2 tsp bicarbonate of soda
25g/1oz medium oatmeal
20g/3/4oz bran
100g/3 1/2oz dark muscovado sugar
50g/2oz unsalted butter (cut into small pieces)
4 tbsps milk (or as needed)

Method

Sift the flour, baking powder, salt and bicarbonate of soda into a mixing bowl. Add the oatmeal, bran and sugar, and mix well to combine.

Add the butter and rub it in with your fingertips until the mixture resembles breadcrumbs. Add 3 tbsps of the milk and stir it in well so the mixture comes together to form a soft dough. If the mixture is a little dry, add the remaining 1 tbsp milk.

Turn the dough out onto a sheet of greaseproof paper and shape it into a log about 25 cm (10inch) long. Wrap the paper round the dough and roll it gently back and forth to make a smooth shape. Twist the ends of the paper together to seal. Chill the dough for about 30 minutes. It can be kept for up to 4 days in the fridge.

Preheat the oven to 190C/375F/Gas mark 5. Unwrap the dough and, using a very sharp knife, cut it across into slices 8 mm (1/3inch) thick. Use the greaseproof paper to line a baking sheet, and place the biscuits on it. Bake for 12 minutes or until lightly browned. Transfer the biscuits to a wire rack and leave to cool completely. They can be kept in an airtight tin for up to 5 days.

Flapjacks (Makes 10)

150g/5oz butter or margarine
100g/3 1/2oz dark brown soft sugar
4 tbsps golden syrup
250g/9oz rolled oats
50g/2oz sultanas or raisins

Method

Preheat the oven to 180C/350F/Gas mark 4. In a saucepan over low heat, combine the butter, brown sugar and golden syrup. Cook, stirring occasionally, until butter and sugar has melted. Stir in the oats and sultanas until coated.

Pour into a 20cm square baking tin. The mixture should be about 2 to 3cm thick. Bake for 30 minutes or until the top is golden. Cut into squares, then leave to cool completely before removing from the tin.

Gingersnaps (Makes 36)

175g/6oz margarine
200g/7oz caster sugar
1 egg
85g/3oz treacle
250g/9oz plain flour
1 tbsp ground ginger
1 tsp ground cinnamon
2 tsps bicarbonate of soda
1/4 tsp salt

Method

Preheat the oven to 180C/350F/Gas mark 4. In a medium bowl, cream together the margarine and sugar until smooth. Beat in the egg and treacle until well blended. Combine the flour, ginger, cinnamon, bicarbonate of soda and salt; stir into the treacle mixture to form a dough.

Roll dough into 2.5cm balls and roll the balls in the remaining sugar. Place biscuits 5cm apart onto ungreased baking trays. Bake for 8 to 10 minutes in the preheated oven. Allow biscuits to cool on baking tray for 5 minutes before removing to a wire rack to cool completely.

Oat & Raisin Cookies (Makes 12)

85g/3oz butter
85g/3oz brown sugar
1 tsp vanilla essence
85g/3oz raisins
50g/2oz sunflower seeds
50g/2oz plain flour
75g/2 1/2oz porridge oats
1/4 tsp bicarbonate of soda
1/2 tsp salt

Method

Preheat the oven to 180C/350F/Gas mark 4. Cream together the butter and sugar until light and fluffy. Stir in the remaining ingredients until completely combined.

Shape into walnut-sized balls and flatten them slightly by pressing down with your hand. Bake for 12-15 minutes or until golden. Cool on a wire rack.

Fig & Walnut Cookie Bars (Makes 40)

Slightly spicy, nutty cookie bars with a rich fig flavour.

200g/7oz caster sugar
3 eggs
100g/3 1/2oz plain flour
1 tsp baking powder
1/8 tsp salt
1/4 tsp ground cloves
1/4 tsp ground cinnamon
1/2 tsp ground allspice
1 tsp vanilla extract
400g/14oz chopped dried figs
100g/3 1/2oz chopped walnuts
100g/3 1/2oz icing sugar (for rolling)

Method

Preheat the oven to 170C/325F/Gas mark 3. Grease and flour a 23x33cm (9x13inch) baking tin. In a large bowl, beat eggs and sugar until thick and pale. Sift together the flour, baking powder, salt, cloves, cinnamon and allspice; blend into the egg mixture along with the vanilla.

Finally fold in the chopped figs and walnuts. Pour the mixture into the prepared tin and spread evenly. Bake for 20 to 25 minutes in the preheated oven, until lightly toasted. When cool, cut into squares and roll in icing sugar.

Raspberry & White Chocolate Cookies

(Makes 24)

225g/8oz unsalted butter (softened)
225g/8oz caster sugar
175g/6oz condensed milk
350g/12oz self-raising flour
150g/5oz white chocolate (chopped)
175g/6oz fresh raspberries

Method

Preheat the oven to 180C/350F/Gas mark 4. In a large bowl, cream the butter and sugar until pale and light and fluffy, and then stir in the condensed milk. Sift in the flour and then work into a soft dough with your hands. Mix in the chocolate.

Take a small handful of dough and flatten with your fingers. Place 2-3 raspberries into the centre of the cookie and fold over the sides of the dough to encase the raspberries.

Repeat with the remaining dough. Place onto parchment lined baking trays, spacing well apart and bake for about 15-18 minutes or until golden brown at the edges, but still a little soft. Leave to cool slightly and set before transferring to a cooling rack.

Marmite® & Cheddar Cookies (Makes 24)

4 tsps Marmite®
225g/8oz of flour
150g/5oz of mature cheddar cheese (grated)
225g/8oz of butter (cut into cubes)
1 large egg
1 egg yolk
2 tbsps double cream

Method

Combine the flour, butter, egg, egg yolk, Marmite® and cream and mix well. Add the grated cheese to the bowl and mix. Turn the dough out on to a floured board and roll into a log. Wrap the log in cling film and chill for at least 2 hours. Preheat the oven to 180C/350F/Gas mark 4. Remove the cling film from the dough and cut into discs, about 1/4inch thick spaced apart on an ungreased baking sheet. Bake for 18 to 25 minutes, or until the cookies are golden and firm to the touch. Cool on a rack.

Parmesan Cheese Biscuits (Makes 8)

150g/5oz freshly grated parmesan
130g/4 1/2 oz butter
150g/5oz flour

Method

Rub together the butter and flour. Add the parmesan. Work into a solid dough. Form a ball and store in the fridge in cling film for at least an hour, or overnight. Roll out the chilled dough between two sheets of parchment to a thickness of 1cm. Use a small biscuit cutter or a glass to cut into round biscuits. Reroll dough and cut further rounds, as many as possible. Place on a baking tray lined with parchment. Bake in a preheated 180C/350F/Gas mark 4 oven for 15 minutes. Cool before serving.

My recipes

Recipe	Chocolate Chip Cookies
Serves	36 (approx.) cookies
Preparation time	10 Mins
Notes/tips	Serve warm with ice cold milk.

Coco powder can be added to make double chocolate chip cookies.

Ingredients

3oz Margarine

3oz caster sugar

3oz brown sugar

1 egg

1/2 tsp Vanilla Essence

8oz Plain Flour

1/4 tsp Bicabof Soda

200g Milk Chocolate
(prefuably Cadbury)

Method

Whisk the margarine, suger and brown sugar together until smooth. Add the egg and vanilla essence. Mix together and then add sieved flour. Chop up the chocolate to chunks and add to mixture. Mix well so the chocolate is evenly distributed. Spoon mixture onto oiled trays with a teaspoon. Place mixture 1 inch away from one another and ensure they're the same size. Place in a preheated oven at 180°C for 10 minutes. Once baked remove from oven and leave 2 minutes before removing from tray. Once removed, place on cooling tray.

My recipes

Recipe _____ Mum's Shortbread _____

Serves _____ 3 dozen squares _____

Preparation time _____ 15 mins _____

Notes/tips

_____
_____
_____
_____

Ingredients

10 oz butter

10 oz plain flour

5 oz cornflour

2 1/2 oz caster sugar

Method

Melt the butter in a saucepan and add all the dry ingredients. Press the mixture evenly into a swiss roll tin. Bake in a preheated oven at 155°C for 25 minutes. Mark off into sections and sprinkle over some caster sugar. Return to the oven at 165°C for a further 10 minutes.

My recipes

Recipe   Honeycomb

Serves   ~

Preparation time 10 mins

Notes/tips   Do not stir!

Ingredients

100g sugar
2 tbsp golden syrup
1 ½ tsp bicarb of soda

Method

Heat sugar and syrup in saucepan until bubbling, add bicarb of soda, stir quickly and turn onto a greased greaseproof paper. Leave to cool and break up when cool.

My recipes

Recipe --

Serves --

Preparation time --

Notes/tips --

Ingredients

------------------------------   ------------------------------

------------------------------   ------------------------------

------------------------------   ------------------------------

------------------------------   ------------------------------

------------------------------   ------------------------------

------------------------------   ------------------------------

------------------------------   ------------------------------

------------------------------   ------------------------------

Method

My recipes

Recipe   --

Serves   ---

Preparation time   ---

Notes/tips   ---

_____

Ingredients

---------------------------------- ----------------------------------

---------------------------------- ----------------------------------

---------------------------------- ----------------------------------

---------------------------------- ----------------------------------

---------------------------------- ----------------------------------

---------------------------------- ----------------------------------

---------------------------------- ----------------------------------

---------------------------------- ----------------------------------

---------------------------------- ----------------------------------

Method

My recipes

Recipe ---

Serves ---

Preparation time ---

Notes/tips ---

Ingredients

---   ---

---   ---

---   ---

---   ---

---   ---

---   ---

---   ---

Method

My recipes

Recipe ....

Serves ....

Preparation time ....

Notes/tips ....

....

....

....

Ingredients

....

....

....

....

....

....

....

....

Method

dessert recipes

Lemon Meringue Pie (Serves 8)

225g/8oz plain white flour
pinch of salt
110g/4oz cold unsalted butter
2 tsps caster sugar
1 medium egg yolk
For the lemon filling
110g/4oz caster sugar
75g/2 1/2oz cornflour
6 egg yolks
4 large lemons, zest and juice
110g/4oz unsalted butter
For the meringue
6 egg whites
300g/10 1/2oz caster sugar

Method

Begin by making the pastry, sieve together the flour and salt into a mixing bowl. Add the butter to the flour and rub between your finger tips until the mixture resembles fine breadcrumbs. Add the sugar to the flour then add the egg yolk with a splash of cold water and mix to form a firm dough. Wrap the pastry in clingfilm and put in the fridge for half an hour. Preheat the oven to 180C/350F/Gas mark 4.

Remove the pastry from the fridge and roll out on a lightly floured surface and line a lightly greased loose bottomed 20cm/8inch fluted flan tin with the pastry. Leave the excess pastry hanging over the sides at this stage. Line the pastry with a disc of baking parchment and fill the paper with baking beans. Now trim away any excess pastry from around the edge with a sharp knife.

Bake the pastry case blind for about 15-20 minutes or until the pastry is lightly golden brown. Remove the paper and the beans for the last 5 minutes cooking. Remove from the oven and leave to cool. Reduce the oven temperature to 150C/300F/Gas mark 2.

To make the filling, mix together the sugar and cornflour in a large bowl and add enough cold water to make a smooth paste. Bring 50ml/2 fl oz of water and the lemon zest to the boil in small pan. Gradually pour the hot liquid over the sugar and cornflour mixture whisking continuously until smooth. Beat in the egg yolks, butter and lemon juice and return to the pan. Cook over a low heat stirring until thickened. Leave to cool slightly then pour into the cooked pastry case and leave to cool.

For the meringue, whisk the egg whites in a large grease free bowl with an electric whisk until they form soft peaks, whisk in the caster sugar, a spoonful at a time continuously whisking on high speed until the meringue has reached stiff peaks and is smooth and glossy.

Transfer the meringue to a piping bag fitted with a star nozzle and pipe the mixture on top of the lemon filling. Alternatively spoon the mixture on top, then using the tip of a knife, lightly flick up the meringue to form little peaks, these will form lovely crispy pieces of meringue as it's baking.

Bake in the preheated oven for about 20-25 minutes until the meringue is lightly golden brown and crisp on the top and soft and marshmallow like on the inside. Remove from the oven, leave to cool on a wire rack.

New York Cheesecake (Serves 8-10)

110g/4oz digestive biscuits
75g/2 1/2oz ginger nut biscuits
50g/2oz dark brown muscovado sugar
50g/2oz unsalted butter, softened
200g/7oz creamy full-fat soft cheese
150g/5oz mascarpone
130ml/4 1/2 fl oz double cream
150g/5oz caster sugar
2 limes, grated zest and juice
1 vanilla pod, split open
3 eggs, separated
1 tbsp icing sugar

Method

Preheat the oven to 170C/325F/Gas mark 3; grease a 21cm springform cake tin. For the base, whiz the biscuits to crumbs in a food processor, then pulse in the muscovado sugar and butter. Press firmly into the base of the tin and chill.

Beat the mascarpone and cream cheese until smooth. Mix in the cream, sugar, lime juice and zest, vanilla seeds from the pod, and the 3 egg yolks. In a separate bowl, whisk the egg whites until stiff. Stir a large spoonful of this into the cheese mixture to loosen it. Gently fold in the rest of the egg whites and pour over the prepared base.

Cook in the oven for 30 minutes, then turn the heat up to 180C/350F/Gas mark 4 for a further 20 minutes. Turn off the heat and leave the cheesecake in the oven for 1 hour to cool and set. Remove from the tin and serve, dusted with the icing sugar; or cover and chill in the tin overnight before serving.

Crème Brûlée (Serves 4)

450ml/16 fl oz double cream
50ml/2 fl oz full fat whole milk
1 vanilla pod, split, seeds removed
5 eggs
75g/2 1/2oz caster sugar, plus 50g/2oz for the top

Method

Preheat the oven to 150C/300F/Gas mark 2.
Pour the cream and milk into a saucepan and bring to a simmer over a medium heat. Take the vanilla pod and using a sharp knife split the pod along the length and scrape out the seeds. Add the seeds to the cream. Do not discard the vanilla pod, this can be simply added to a jar of sugar to create a wonderfully flavoured vanilla sugar which can be used at a later date.

Separate the eggs, only the yolks are used in this recipe, the whites can be used in another dish or frozen for use at a later date. Whisk together the egg yolks and sugar until well combined. When the cream and milk mixture is coming to a simmer, pour it into the bowl with the egg yolks and sugar and stir thoroughly to combine all the ingredients and dissolve the sugar.

If you wish, the mixture can be strained through a fine sieve to ensure the mixture is totally smooth. Carefully ladle the cream and egg mixture into 4 individual ramekins, then place them into a deep baking tray and fill the tray with hot water until it reaches half way up the sides of the ramekins.

Place the water filled tray (this is called a Bain Marie) into the preheated oven and cook for about half an hour, or until the custard is set firm but still with a slight wobble. Remove the tray from the oven and take out the ramekins and allow to cool completely. To finish the dish, liberally sprinkle the extra caster sugar in an even layer over the top of the cooled custard. If you have a blowtorch, heat the surface of the sugar until the sugar caramelises and is deep golden brown and has formed a lovely crunchy layer. Alternatively, heat under the highest possible setting under the grill.

Sticky Toffee Pudding

(Serves 4-6)

400g/14oz prunes, stones removed
500ml/18 fl oz water
1 tsp vanilla extract
110g/4oz butter, softened
350g/12oz dark muscovado sugar
1 tbsp black treacle
1 tbsp golden syrup
4 eggs
1 tbsp bicarbonate of soda
400g/14oz self raising flour
For the sauce
500ml/18 fl oz double cream
175g/6oz demerara sugar
175g/6oz butter, softened
1 tbsp golden syrup
1 tbsp treacle

Method

Preheat the oven to 190C/375F/Gas mark 5. Line a 20cm/8inch cake tin with baking parchment paper. Place the prunes in a saucepan, add the water, bring to the boil, reduce the heat and simmer for 2-3 minutes. Stir in the vanilla extract, then blend until thick and smooth. Place the sugar and butter in a large bowl and beat together until smooth, light and fluffy. Stir in the treacle and golden syrup. Sieve the flour into the bowl and mix well to combine. Break the eggs into the mixture one at a time, stirring well after each addition.

Add the bicarbonate of soda to the prune mix, then pour this mixture into the flour mixture and beat well with a wooden spoon until the ingredients are all thoroughly combined. Transfer the mixture to the prepared cake tin and bake for 1-1 1/2 hours in the preheated until well risen and springy to the touch. To make the sauce, place the cream in a saucepan and heat gently, add the sugar and butter and stir until dissolved, then stir in the treacle and golden syrup. Simmer for a few minutes stirring thoroughly until the sauce is smooth and silky.

Remove the pudding from the oven, spoon into warmed serving bowls and serve the sauce poured over the top. This pudding is simply delicious served on its own, but try serving it with a generous scoop of vanilla ice cream or cream over the top.

Individual Fruit Crumble

(Serves 4)

Soft fruits make lovely crumbles, their juices bubbling up through the sugary topping. Make them in individual dishes and serve with scoops of vanilla ice cream.

110g/4oz blueberries
110g/4oz blackberries
200g/7oz raspberries
110g/4oz demerara sugar, plus a little extra to top
75g/2 1/2oz plain flour
75g/2 1/2oz unsalted butter, slightly softened
50g/2oz porridge oats

Method

Preheat the oven to 200C/400F/Gas mark 6. Lightly grease the sides of 4 x 225ml ovenproof ramekins or bowls and place on a baking sheet. In a bowl, mix all the berries together with 50g/2oz of the sugar and divide between the dishes, pressing down gently.

Put the flour in a bowl and add the butter, cut into pieces. Rub in with your fingertips until the mixture just starts to bind together. Stir in the remaining sugar and the oats to make a coarse crumble. Scatter the mixture over the fruits, piling it up in the centre as it will sink after baking. Sprinkle with extra sugar. Bake for about 30 minutes until the crumble is golden and the fruits have started to bubble up.

Soft Centred Chocolate Pudding (Serves 8)

A stunning sexy little number, a delicious chocolate pudding with a liquid centre.

250g/9oz 66% cocoa quality dark chocolate
250g/9oz butter
8 egg yolks
4 egg whites
110g/4oz caster sugar
4 tsps rice or cornflour
For the filling
50ml/2 fl oz hot expresso or strong black coffee
150ml/5 fl oz milk chocolate

Method

Begin by making the liquid filling by melting the chocolate in the hot coffee and pouring into ice cube trays to about 3/4 full. Freeze until required. Preheat the oven to 180C/350F/Gas mark 4.

Generously butter 8 individual souffle moulds and set aside. Melt the dark chocolate with the butter in a bowl over a pan of gently simmering water, remove from the heat and set aside. Beat together the egg yolks and sugar until light and fluffy then combine with the melted chocolate.

Whisk the egg whites to soft peaks then fold in the melted chocolate. Sift the flour into the mixture. Spoon the mixture into the moulds to come to about 1/4 full, then unmould the chocolate ice cubes and place one in the centre of each pudding. Now fill the moulds up to 3/4 full with the chocolate mix.

Bake in the oven for 10-12 minutes until the puddings rise. Remove from the oven and leave to rest for a couple of minutes then turn out onto a serving plate. Dust with cocoa powder or icing sugar to serve.

Bread & Butter Pudding (Serves 6)

50g/2oz butter softened, plus extra for greasing
750g/1lb 10oz thick sliced white bread, crusts removed
75g/2 1/2oz sultanas
For the custard filling
12 egg yolks
110g/4oz caster sugar
450ml/16 fl oz full fat milk
450ml/16 fl oz double cream
1 vanilla pod, split, seeds scraped out

Method

Grease a 25cm x 23cm/10inch x 9inch (3inch/7cm depth) ovenproof dish with softened butter. Preheat the oven to 150C/300F/Gas mark 2. Butter all the bread slices on both sides, then cut into half to form triangles. Arrange a layer of bread slices in the bottom of the dish, slightly overlapping the slices. Sprinkle over half of the sultanas, then repeat the process with more bread slices and the remaining sultanas. Finish with a layer of bread slices, then set aside.

To make the custard filling, bring the cream, milk, vanilla pod and seeds to the boil in a large saucepan. Meanwhile whisk together the egg yolks and sugar together in a separate bowl until pale fluffy. When the cream mixture has come to the boil, remove from the heat, discard the vanilla pod (this can be dried and used later in another recipe) then pour the hot cream over the beaten egg yolks whisking continuously until the mixture is smooth and well combined. Strain the cream mixture through a sieve over the layers of bread, then set aside for 20 minutes to allow the mixture to soak into the bread.

Fill a separate large baking dish with boiling water up to about 1 inch in depth, then place the prepared oven proof dish into the water, this method of cooking (Bain Marie) will allow the pudding to be cooked more gently. Place into the preheated oven for 45 minutes to 1 hour, or until the custard has just set. The custard should still just be slightly moist in the centre and the top of the pudding beautifully golden brown.

Rice Pudding (Serves 4-6)

Such a simple pudding to prepare, but so delicious, soft sweet plump rice lightly spiced with nutmeg with a scrumptious skin on top of the pudding.

110g/4oz pudding rice
400g/14oz evaporated milk
570ml/20 fl oz/1 pint full fat milk
50g/2oz caster sugar
25g/1oz butter
grated nutmeg

Method

Preheat the oven to 150C/300F/Gas mark 2. Grease a 23cm/9inch ovenproof dish with a depth of 3cm/1 1/4 inches with softened butter. Place the rice and sugar in the buttered oven proof dish, combine the evaporated milk with the full fat milk in a jug and pour over the rice and sugar.

Give the mixture a good stir, then generously grate over some freshly grated nutmeg, then finally dot the butter on top in little flecks. Place the dish in the preheated oven for 30 minutes then give the rice a really good stir.

Repeat the stirring after another 30 minutes, then pop it back into the oven for a further hour this time without stirring. The rice will be beautifully plump and tender with a delicious skin on top. Remove from the oven and serve.

This pudding is lovely served with some stewed fruits such as plums, or alternatively, add a good spoon full of strawberry or raspberry jam and stir through.

Queen of Puddings (Serves 4)

3 large eggs separated
grated zest of 1 lemon
75g/2 1/2oz caster sugar, plus extra for sprinkling
110g/4oz fresh white breadcrumbs
3 tbsps raspberry jam
570ml/20 fl oz/1 pint milk
butter for greasing

Method

Preheat the oven to 180C/350F/Gas mark 4. Place the milk in a saucepan and bring to the boil, remove from the heat, add the lemon zest, breadcrumbs and half the sugar,stir well to combine then set aside for 20 minutes to allow the breadcrumbs to swell. Lightly beat the egg yolks, then incorporate into the cooled milk and breadcrumb mixture.

Pour the mixture into a greased 1 1/2 pint/850ml shallow pie dish, bake in the centre of the preheated oven for 25-30 minutes or until just lightly set. Remove from the oven, leave to cool slightly, then carefully but evenly spread the raspberry jam over the top of the pudding. (Heating the raspberry jam slightly will make it easier to spread).

Meanwhile beat the egg whites in a scrupulously clean bowl until it forms soft peaks, then gradually add the remaining sugar, continue whisking until the meringue mixture is stiff.

Spread the meringue over the top of the pudding, then using the tip of a knife or the prongs of a fork, form the meringue into small peaks which will turn lovely and sticky during cooking. Sprinkle a teaspoon of sugar on top of the meringue, then bake for 10-15 minutes until lightly golden brown.

My recipes

Recipe	Mum's Chocolate Sauce
Serves	1 pint
Preparation time	15 mins
Notes/tips	Serve warm or cold

with all puddings.

Ingredients

2tbsp Cocoa

14oz milk chocolate

1 oz butter

1/2 pint of water

Method

Stir water in cocoa and bring
to the boil, slowly stirring constantly.
Leave to simmer for 1 minute
until smooth. Remove from heat
and stir in the chocolate. When
the sauce is smooth beat in
the butter with a wooden spoon.

My recipes

Recipe --

Serves --

Preparation time ---

Notes/tips --

Ingredients

--   --

--   --

--   --

--   --

--   --

--   --

--   --

Method

My recipes

Recipe   --

Serves   --

Preparation time   --

Notes/tips   --

Ingredients

--------------------------- ---------------------------

--------------------------- ---------------------------

--------------------------- ---------------------------

--------------------------- ---------------------------

--------------------------- ---------------------------

--------------------------- ---------------------------

--------------------------- ---------------------------

--------------------------- ---------------------------

Method

My recipes

Recipe   --

Serves   --

Preparation time   --

Notes/tips   --

Ingredients

--   --

--   --

--   --

--   --

--   --

--   --

--   --

--   --

Method

My recipes

Recipe ---

Serves ---

Preparation time ---

Notes/tips ---

Ingredients

--------------------- ---------------------

--------------------- ---------------------

--------------------- ---------------------

--------------------- ---------------------

--------------------- ---------------------

--------------------- ---------------------

--------------------- ---------------------

--------------------- ---------------------

Method

My recipes

Recipe --

Serves --

Preparation time --

Notes/tips --

Ingredients

-- --

-- --

-- --

-- --

-- --

-- --

-- --

-- --

Method

My recipes

Recipe --

Serves --

Preparation time --

Notes/tips --

Ingredients --

---------------------------- ----------------------------

---------------------------- ----------------------------

---------------------------- ----------------------------

---------------------------- ----------------------------

---------------------------- ----------------------------

---------------------------- ----------------------------

---------------------------- ----------------------------

---------------------------- ----------------------------

Method

pastry recipes

Shortcrust Pastry

The type of fat used to make shortcrust pastry is a personal choice, I love to use purely butter as it creates a rich deep flavoured pastry, however it is possible to use half butter and half lard. One rule to remember is the fat you choose should always be at room temperature. It is important to rub the fat into the flour as quickly as possible, otherwise if the fat is cold it will take longer to incorporate and the fat will become oily. Generally speaking, the amount of fat you use in shortcrust pastry is half the amount of flour, so for 110g/4oz flour you use 50g/2oz of fat.

The flour should always be plain, and also ensure the flour is well within the best before date; I have found that stale flour does not make the best pastry. I always add a pinch of salt to the flour even it is to be used for sweet dishes.

To begin the pastry, sift the flour and a pinch of salt into a bowl, holding the sieve high above the bowl so that you incorporate as much air into the pastry. Cut the fat into small lumps and add to the flour. Using a knife, cut the fat into the flour until the mixture is evenly blended, then using your fingertips, and being as light and gentle as possible, rub the fat into the flour. Lift it up high and let it fall back down into the bowl, which again means air is being incorporated all the time and this is what makes the pastry light. Speed is also what's needed here, rub the mixture just long enough to make it crumbly with just a few odd lumps.

The next step is to add water, and the water must be as cold as possible. Exact amounts can never be specified because the amount of water the flour absorbs varies so much.

Too much water will make the pastry sticky and difficult to roll out; on the other hand, too little will result in the pastry being also difficult to roll out and the pastry will be too crumbly. Start with about 1 tbsp of ice cold water, sprinkling it evenly all around. Then with a knife, start bringing the dough together, cutting and turning it to make a start, then continue using your fingertips. Add more water, little by little, if you need it.

All the bits of fat and flour should be incorporated and the pastry should leave the sides of the bowl clean. If this hasn't happened, then keep adding a touch more water to bring the mix together.

All pastry must be rested before rolling out. Flour contains something called gluten which reacts to the water in a way which, given time, makes the dough more elastic in texture and easier to roll out. Wrap the pastry in clingfilm and place in the fridge for at least 30 minutes to allow the pastry to rest.

Making pastry in advance is perfectly acceptable; it will keep for up to 3 days in the fridge quite happily. Always remember to bring the pastry back to room temperature before rolling out. Pastry will also keep in the freezer for up to 3 months.

Sweet Pastry

225g/8oz plain white flour
pinch of salt
110g/4oz cold unsalted butter
2 tsps caster sugar
1 medium egg yolk

Method

Sieve the flour into a bowl. Add the salt and butter to the flour and rub between your fingertips until the mixture resembles fine breadcrumbs.

Add the sugar to the flour then add the egg yolk with a splash of cold water and mix to form a firm dough. Wrap the pastry in clingfilm and chill in the fridge for half an hour.

Rough Puff Pastry

450g/1lb plain flour
large pinch of salt
375g/13 oz cold butter, cut into 2cm/3/4inch pieces
250ml/9 fl oz cold water
1 tbsp lemon juice

Method

Sift the flour and salt into a large bowl and add the butter. Mix the butter around in the bowl with a large metal spoon to coat in the flour. Mix the cold water and lemon juice together in a jug and pour into the flour and butter mixture. Using a round tipped knife, cut across the contents of the bowl, turning the bowl continuously as you chop the butter into the flour until the dough comes together.

When the dough has come together as a loose lump, tip it out onto a lightly floured work surface and quickly shape it into a large slab about the size of a standard house brick. Flour the surface well and roll out the dough to form a rectangle, appropriately 38cm/15inch x 20cm/8inch.

Fold one-third of the dough into the centre, then fold the other third over that. Roll the pastry out again to the same dimensions and fold once more as before.

Rotate the dough a quarter turn and repeat the folding and rolling process a further 3-4 times, rotating the dough a quarter turn between each roll and fold. Don't worry if the butter starts to ooze through the dough occasionally in the early stages, just keep the board and rolling pin well floured. After the final rolling stage, wrap the pastry in cling film and place onto a baking sheet and chill in the fridge for several hours or preferably overnight for the butter to firm up and the pastry to relax.

When ready to use, if the pastry is very firm, allow it to sit at room temperature for 5 minutes before rolling out and use as required. The pastry will freeze very well for up to six weeks.

Choux Pastry

Choux Pastry is a very light twice cooked pastry usually used for sweet desserts and buns such as eclairs, profiteroles and choux puffs. It is also the base of a classic French dessert called Gateau St. Honore and the dramatic and impressive Croquembouche, a pyramid shaped dessert made up of lots of sweet filled choux buns coated in caramel, often served as an alternative to a traditional wedding cake. Choux Pastry can also be used for savoury dishes such as Gougeres, a large ring of choux buns flavoured with Gruyere or Emmental cheese. The pastry is so versatile, it can also be deep fried to create both sweet and savoury small crisp fritters called Beignets. Choux Pastry has a reputation for being rather difficult to master, however once you know the technique it is really quite straight forward. The pastry has a high water content. The water in the mixture creates steam during the cooking process which forces the pastry to expand in volume, leaving it with a hollow centre and a light texture. A preheated oven is essential to raise and set the choux pastry, if you take it out of the oven before it's firm to the touch and cooked thoroughly it will collapse. Any filling should not be added until the last possible minute as this will make the pastry soggy.

Basic Choux Pastry

110g/4oz plain flour, sieved
150ml/5 fl oz water
75g/2 1/2oz butter
3 eggs, beaten

Method

Place the water and butter into a saucepan over a medium high heat and stir with a wooden spoon until the butter melts. Allow the mixture to come to a rolling boil and remove the pan from the heat.

Add the sieved flour and beat vigorously with the wooden spoon until the mixture forms a thick paste. Reduce the heat slightly and return the pan to the heat, stirring continually and beating vigorously for about a minute. The mixture will leave the sides of the pan clean. Remove the pan from the heat and allow to cool slightly.

Pour a quarter of the beaten eggs into the mixture and, using the wooden spoon beat very well until the egg is incorporated into the mixture. Continue to add the eggs, beating vigorously between each addition.

The mixture will have softened with a smooth, shiny and silky appearance with a dropping consistency. You may not need to use all the eggs or you may need a little extra. If the mix is too stiff with not enough egg, then the pastry will be too heavy; but if the mixture is too wet with too much egg, they will not hold their shape.

Profiteroles & Chocolate Sauce (Serves 4)

basic choux pastry mix (previous page)
For the filling
280ml/10 fl oz double cream, lightly whipped
For the chocolate sauce
110g/4oz dark chocolate
2 tbsps double cream
small knob of unsalted butter

Method

Preheat the oven to 200C/400F/Gas mark 6. Line a baking tray with a sheet of baking parchment or greaseproof paper. Place the choux pastry into a piping bag fitted with a plain 1cm plain round nozzle and carefully pipe small rounds of the mixture onto the baking paper, leaving enough room between each one to allow the pastry to expand. If you do not have a piping bag, simply spoon heaped tsps of the mixture onto the tray.

Just prior to placing the tray into the oven, dot the baking tray with a little cold water, this will create steam, allowing the pastry to rise. Cook the buns for about 10 minutes or until well risen and golden brown.

Turn off the oven and leave in the oven for a further 5 minutes to allow the buns to dry out. Remove from the oven and cool completely on a wire rack. When the buns are completely cold, make a small incision in the base of the buns, spoon the whipped cream into a piping bag and pipe the cream into the hole and fill the cavity of the bun. Alternatively cut a small incision into the sides of the buns and spoon the cream in with a tsp.

Place the chocolate, butter and double cream into a bowl over a pan of very gently simmering water and allow the chocolate to melt. Do not allow the bowl to touch the water. Gently stir until the chocolate has melted and the mixture is smooth and glossy. Arrange the filled profiteroles onto a serving plate and drizzle over the warm chocolate sauce.

Treacle Tart (Serves 6)

A pastry lined tart with a filling of golden syrup and breadcrumbs, lightly spiced with ginger and a burst of lemon zest.

225g/8oz plain flour, sieved
110g/4oz butter, chilled and diced
1 medium egg, lightly beaten
For the filling
450g/1lb golden syrup
75g/2 1/2oz fresh white breadcrumbs
generous pinch of ground ginger
1 lemon, zest finely grated, plus 2 tbsps of the juice

Method

Preheat the oven to 190C/375F/Gas mark 5. In a large mixing bowl, rub the chilled butter into the sieved flour until it resembles fine breadcrumbs, mix in the egg with a knife, then on a lightly floured surface form to create a smooth dough. Wrap the pastry in cling film and set aside to rest in the fridge for half an hour.

Roll out the pastry on a lightly floured surface to line a 23cm/9inch loose bottomed tart tin, leaving any excess pastry hanging over the sides of the tin, this can be trimmed off after baking. Prick the base of the tart all over with a fork.

Line the pastry base with parchment paper, then weigh down with rice or ceramic baking beans. Bake the pastry blind for 10-15 minutes, remove the paper and beans and return to the oven for a few more minutes until light golden brown. Leave to cool slightly, then using a sharp knife trim away any excess pastry from around the edges to create a neat edge to the tart.

Mix together the filling ingredients in a large bowl and pour into the pastry case. (Tip: warming the syrup first will make it easier to combine all the ingredients). Return to the oven and bake for approximately 30 minutes.

Bakewell Tart (Serves 8)

A delicious jam and almond sponge flavoured tart.

425g/15oz plain flour
1 egg, beaten
175g/6oz caster sugar
2 egg yolk
250g/9oz butter
pinch of salt
50g/2oz ground almonds
For the filling
400g/14oz ground almonds
175g/6oz caster sugar
8 eggs beaten
1/2 tsp almond essence
3 tbsps raspberry jam
50g/2oz flaked almonds
icing sugar to dust

Method

For the pastry, place the flour, salt, sugar, butter and almonds into a food processor and pulse until the mixture resembles breadcrumbs. Add the eggs and egg yolks one at a time until a smooth dough is formed. Wrap the dough in cling film then chill in the fridge for half an hour.

Preheat the oven to 180C/350F/Gas mark 4. Grease a 23cm/9inch loose bottomed tart tin. Roll out the dough and line the tart tin, leaving any excess hanging over the sides. Prick the base of the tart with a fork, then line the tart with parchment paper and baking beans, bake blind for 15 minutes.

Remove from the oven, remove the paper and beans, then return to the oven for a few more minutes to allow the pastry to dry out and become lightly golden brown. Remove from the oven, leave to cool slightly, then using a sharp knife, trim any excess pastry from the sides to create a neat edge. Reduce the oven temperature to 170C/325F/Gas mark 3.

Meanwhile for the filling, mix together the ground almonds and sugar in a large mixing bowl, add the beaten eggs and almond essence and mix well. Spread the jam over the base of the cooled pastry tart then pour the filling mixture over the jam to fill the pastry case.

Sprinkle the flaked almonds over the top of the tart, then bake in the oven for 25-30 minutes, or until the filling is cooked through and the top is golden brown. Remove from the oven, allow to cool slightly, dust the top the tart with icing sugar then cut into slices, serve warm or cold with custard or cream.

Tarte Au Citron (Serves 8)

A classic French lemon tart.

175g/6oz plain flour
110g/4oz cold butter
25g/1oz icing sugar
1 egg yolk
1 tbsp cold water
For the lemon filling
5 eggs
130ml/4 1/2 fl oz double cream
225g/8oz caster sugar
4 lemons, juice and zest
icing sugar for dusting

Method

Begin by making the pastry, sieve the flour and icing sugar into a mixing bowl or food processor, add the butter and mix until it resembles fine breadcrumbs. Add the egg yolk and water to create a smooth dough. Knead the pastry lightly then wrap in clingfilm and chill in the fridge for 20 minutes. Grease a 23cm/9inch loose bottomed, fluted flan tin.

Remove the pastry from the fridge and roll out on a lightly floured surface large enough to line the flan tin. Carefully roll up the pastry over the rolling pin, then un-roll the pastry over the tin, gently easing the pastry into the base and sides of the tin. Any overhanging pastry can be left at this stage, hanging over the sides of the tin. If the pastry has cracked, don't worry, simply press it together to seal.

Carefully press the pastry into the flutes of the tin, then lightly prick the base of the pastry with a fork but not quite all the way through. Preheat the oven to 200C/400F/Gas mark 6. Place the lined tin onto a baking tray, cover with clingfilm and chill in the fridge for 20 minutes. Remove the clingfilm and line the pastry case with baking parchment or tin foil. Fill the tin with baking beans and blind bake for 12-15 minutes, until the pastry is set, then lift out the foil and beans.

Using a sharp knife, carefully trim the excess pastry from the overhanging sides to create a neat finish. Return the trimmed empty pastry case to the oven for a further 8-10 minutes, or until pale golden in colour and completely dry and crisp. Remove from the oven and set aside to cool on a wire rack. Reduce the oven temperature to 170C/325F/Gas mark 3.

To make the lemon filling, lightly whisk the eggs in a large bowl, then add the remainder of the filling ingredients and whisk until well combined. Pour the mixture into a jug, then fill the cooled pastry case. To prevent it from spilling, only add two-thirds of the mixture at this stage. Carefully sit the baking sheet and tart on the oven shelf, then top up with the remaining filling to completely fill it.

Bake in the oven for 25-30 minutes, or until just set but still retaining a slight wobble in the centre. Remove from the oven and leave to cool slightly. When the tart seems firm enough, remove the tart from the tin. The easiest way to do this is to place the base of the tin onto a can and let the outer ring fall to the works surface. Carefully remove the base, dust the top of the tart with sieved icing sugar and transfer to a large serving plate. Cut into slices and serve slightly warm or cold.

Crème Anglaise (Serves 2)

Nothing can beat the taste of rich smooth vanilla flavoured home made custard poured generously over your favourite pudding

2 free range egg yolks
280ml/10 fl oz full fat cream milk
2 tbsps caster sugar
1 vanilla pod, seeds removed

Method

Heat the milk, vanilla pod and seeds in a saucepan until almost boiling. Beat the egg yolks with the sugar in a large bowl until well combined.

Slowly pour the hot milk over the egg and sugar mixture, stirring continuously until thoroughly combined. Remove the vanilla pod, but do not discard, this can be washed and dried, then placed into a jar with some caster sugar, which will create vanilla flavoured sugar to be used at a later date.

Return the mixture to a clean saucepan and heat over a low to medium heat, stirring continuously, until the mixture starts to thicken and is thick enough to coat the back of a spoon. Remove from the heat, strain through a sieve and serve.

Crème Patissière (Makes 450ml/16 fl oz)

Pastry cream is a rich sweet cream which can be used to fill fruit tarts, doughnuts and choux pastries and any other number of sweet treats. This basic recipe can be flavoured with coffee, nuts, caramel and chocolate, in fact almost anything, just use this basic recipe and let your imagination run wild.

4 egg yolks
110g/4oz caster sugar
25g/1oz plain flour
1 vanilla pod or 1/2 tsp vanilla extract
350ml/12 fl oz full fat milk

Method

Split the vanilla pod lengthways with a sharp knife and scrape out the seeds. Place the milk into a saucepan together with the vanilla pod and seeds and bring slowly up to the boil.

In a separate bowl, whisk together the egg yolks, sugar and flour until well combined and smooth. Remove the vanilla pod from the milk, do not discard, this can be dried and added to a jar of sugar to create a wonderful vanilla flavoured sugar. If using vanilla extract, this can be added to the warm milk as it is coming up to the boil.

Pour the milk over the beaten egg mixture, whisking continually, return the mixture to the pan and stir over a low heat until the mixture thickens and is smooth. This should take about 2 minutes. If the mixture looks a little lumpy, simply whisk vigorously. Remove from the heat, if the mixture still looks a little lumpy, strain the cream through a fine sieve into a clean bowl. Lay a piece of clingfilm over the surface of the cream, this will stop a skin forming.

Beef & Chorizo Pie (Serves 4)

3 tbsps olive oil
1kg/2.2lb braising beef, trimmed and cut into chunks
200g/7oz chorizo, cut into chunks
2 red onions, peeled and cut into wedges
3 cloves garlic, crushed
pinch dried chilli flakes
250ml/9 fl oz red wine
500ml/18 fl oz beef stock
2 sprigs fresh thyme
1 small bay leaf
1 x 400g/14oz tin chopped tomatoes
1 tbsp butter, softened
1 tbsp plain flour, plus extra for rolling out
450g/1lb puff pastry
1 egg, beaten

Method

Heat 1 tbsp of olive oil in a large pan. Season the beef and brown in batches.
Set aside. Add extra oil and brown the chorizo. Set aside. Add the onions,
cook for a few minutes, then add the garlic and chilli and cook for a minute.
Return the meat to the pan and pour in the red wine. Simmer for a minute
then add the stock, thyme, bay leaf and tin of tomatoes. Bring to the boil,
then reduce, cover and simmer for an hour.

Take off the heat and remove the bay leaf and thyme sprigs. Let cool. Skim
any fat from the surface, return to the heat and bring to a gentle boil. In a
small pan, melt the butter and stir in the flour to make a roux. Stir into the
main dish until the sauce thickens, then pour the filling into a pie dish.

Preheat the oven to 190C/375F/Gas mark 5. Roll out the pastry on a floured
surface, so that it's slightly larger than the pie dish. Brush the rim with water
and top with the pastry lid. Press down to seal. Brush with beaten egg and cut
a steam vent in the top. Place on a baking tray and cook for about 40
minutes, until puffed and golden.

Cornish Pasties (Serves 4-6)

450g/1lb plain flour, plus extra for dusting
2 tsps baking powder
1 tsp salt
130g/4 1/2 oz unsalted butter
2 egg yolks
130ml/4 1/2 fl oz cold water
For the filling
300g/10 1/2oz braising steak, finely chopped
1 tbsp plain flour
150g/5oz onion, peeled, finely sliced
150g/5oz swede, peeled, finely sliced
450g/1lb potato, peeled, finely sliced
50g/2oz butter
salt and freshly ground black pepper
1 egg, beaten for glazing

Method

Begin by making the pastry, sieve the flour, baking powder and salt into a large mixing bowl, rub in the butter using your finger tips until the mixture resembles fine breadcrumbs. Add the eggs yolks and a little of the water until the mixture comes together to form a dough. You may not need all the water, so add a little at a time. Wrap the pastry in clingfilm and chill in the fridge for half an hour.

Place the chopped beef into a bowl, then add the flour and mix until the meat is well coated. Season with salt and lots of freshly ground black pepper. Add the sliced vegetables and mix to combine all the ingredients.

Preheat the oven to 180C/350F/Gas mark 4. Remove the pastry from the fridge, then roll out on a lightly floured surface. Using a large plate as a template, cut out the pastry into discs. Divide the filling onto the pastry rounds, making sure there is a gap around the edges of the pastry. Brush the pastry edges with the beaten egg, then carefully bring the pastry up from the sides and over the top to encase the filling.

Using your fingertips crimp and twist the top of the pastry to create a twisted plaited edge. Brush the pasties with the beaten egg, place on a lightly greased baking sheet and bake in the preheated oven for 45 minutes, or until the pastry is beautifully golden brown. Remove from the oven, leave to rest for 10 minutes then serve.

Quiche Lorraine (Serves 6-8)

50g/2oz butter, cut into small pieces
50g/2oz lard, cut into small pieces
200g/7oz self raising flour
pinch of salt
2-3 tbsps ice cold water
For the filling
8-10 thin rashers streaky bacon, roughly chopped
4 egg yolks
2 eggs
400ml/14 fl oz double cream
50g/2oz cheddar cheese, grated
freshly grated nutmeg

Method

For the pastry, place the butter, lard, flour and salt into a food processor and blend until the mixture resembles fine breadcrumbs. Turn the pastry out into a mixing bowl and, using a round bladed knife, stir in enough ice cold water to bind the mixture together. Lightly knead the dough until well combined, dust with a little flour and wrap in clingfilm and chill in the fridge for 30 minutes.

Meanwhile preheat the oven to 180C/350F/Gas mark 4. Roll out the pastry on a lightly floured surface as thinly as possible. Line a 20cm/ 8inch fluted loose bottomed flan tin. Lightly prick the base of the pastry with a fork and line the pastry with baking parchment and fill with baking beans. Place the tin on a baking tray and bake blind for 15-20 minutes. Remove the paper and beans and continue baking until the pastry is pale golden brown and cooked through.

To make the filling, fry the bacon in a medium hot frying pan with a drizzle of oil until crisp. Remove the bacon pieces and drain on absorbent kitchen paper to remove any excess oil.

Whisk the egg yolks and eggs together in a bowl, stir in the cream, season with salt, pepper and some freshly grated nutmeg. Stir in two-thirds of the grated cheese and the bacon pieces, mix well to combine. Pour the filling into the pastry case and sprinkle the remaining cheese on the top.

Bake in the preheated oven for 30-40 minutes, or until the tart is golden brown and nicely puffed up and the custard filling is just set. Remove from the oven, leave to cool slightly and serve at room temperature or leave to cool completely and serve cold.

Main course *(crossed out text)*

My recipes

Recipe — Pork Satay

Serves — 5/6 portions

Preparation time — 1/2 hour

Notes/tips — Pork can be swapped for chicken.

Ingredients

2 pound Pork peices

1 onion

1 red pepper

amoy peanut satay (1/2)

thai red curry paste (1/2 tsp)

a splash of cream

(add water if dries out).

Brown the meat in pan with oil
Add the vegetables and leave to
simmer for 8-10 minutes. Add
the peanut satay and curry
paste. Leave simmering, if dries
out add water. Just before
serving stir in the cream.
Serve with noodles or rice.

Recipe   Perfect Cocktail Sausages

Serves   ~

Preparation time   2 mins

Notes/tips

Ingredients

Cocktail Sausages
Seseme Seed Oil
Soy Sauce
Honey

Method

Coat the sausages with
ingredients in a pan tray and
cook in the oven.

My recipes

Recipe ....

Serves ....

Preparation time ....

Notes/tips ....

....

....

....

Ingredients ....

....

....

....

....

....

....

....

Method

My recipes

Recipe ....

Serves ....

Preparation time ....

Notes/tips ....

....

....

....

Ingredients ....

....

....

....

....

....

....

....

Method

My recipes

Recipe ....

Serves ....

Preparation time ....

Notes/tips ....

....

....

....

Ingredients ....

....

....

....

....

....

....

....

Method

My recipes

Recipe ....

Serves ....

Preparation time ....

Notes/tips ....

....

....

....

....

Ingredients ....

....

....

....

....

....

....

....

....

Method

My recipes

Recipe ....

Serves ....

Preparation time ....

Notes/tips ....

....

....

....

Ingredients ....

....

....

....

....

....

....

....

Method

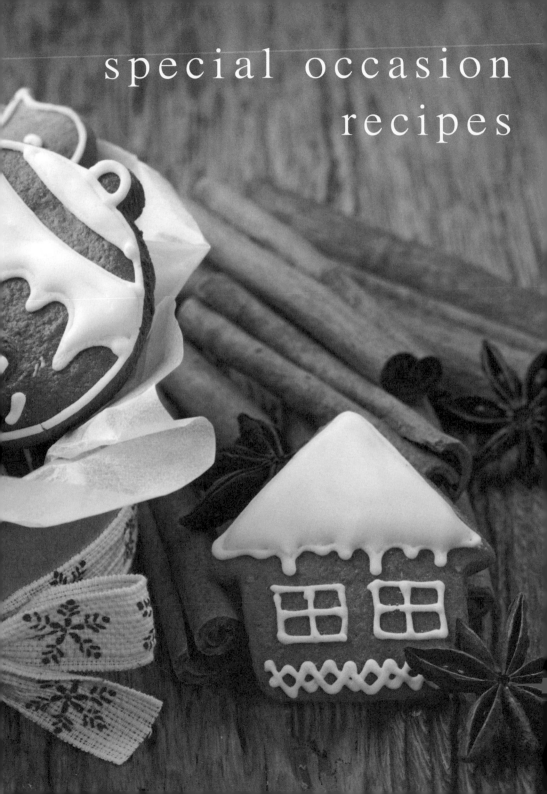

special occasion
recipes

Stollen (Serves 10-12)

A traditional German recipe. A marzipan filled yeast dough packed with dried fruits, a wonderful alternative to the traditional Christmas Cake.

2 tsps dried yeast
225g/8oz plain flour
100ml/3 1/2 fl oz warm milk
pinch of salt
1 tsp caster sugar
1 tsp ground mixed spice
200g/7oz dried mixed fruit
50g/2oz glace cherries, chopped
25g/1oz flaked almonds
50g/2oz butter
1 egg
250g/9oz marzipan
To finish
25g/1oz melted butter
50g/2oz icing sugar

Method

Place the warm milk and yeast into a bowl and mix well, set aside for the yeast to work for about 6-8 minutes. Meanwhile, sift together the flour, salt and mixed spice into a large bowl.

Add the dried fruit, cherries, almonds and butter and mix well to combine. Add the yeast mixture together with the egg and mix well to combine all the ingredients to form a dough.

Knead the dough on a lightly floured surface for 4-5 minutes, place the dough in a bowl, cover with a sheet of clingfilm and set aside in a warm place to prove for 25 minutes. Uncover the dough and turn out onto a work surface lightly dusted with flour. Knock the dough back to reduce the volume, then once again knead the dough for a further 5 minutes.

Push and roll out the dough by hand into a flat oval shape about 23x18cm/9x7inch in size. Roll out the marzipan into a piece about 18x5cm/7x2inch. Place the marzipan in the centre of the dough, then fold over the sides of the dough to seal in the marzipan. Place the dough seal side down onto a greased baking tray lined with parchment, cover and set aside somewhere warm to prove for an hour. Preheat the oven to 180C/350F/Gas mark 4.

Bake for 40-45 minutes or until well risen and golden brown. Remove the stollen from the oven, brush with the melted butter and dust liberally with the sifted icing sugar.

Mince Pies (Makes 12)

450g/1lb plain flour
1 tsp baking powder
250g/9oz butter
50g/2oz caster sugar
2 egg yolks
beaten egg to seal and glaze and icing sugar to finish
For the mincemeat
110g/4oz raisins
110g/4oz sultanas
110g/4oz currants
1 cooking apple, peeled, cored and chopped
1 lemon
75g/2 1/2oz mixed peel
110g/4oz suet
110g/4oz dark brown muscovado sugar
1 tsp ground cinnamon
1/2 tsp ground nutmeg
1 tsp ground mixed spice
1/2 tsp ground ginger
50ml/2 fl oz brandy
50ml/2 fl oz sherry

Method

To prepare the mincemeat, begin by placing the whole lemon in a small saucepan, cover with water and simmer gently for an hour. Leave to cool, then cut in half, remove the pips and cut into small pieces including the rind.

In a large mixing bowl mix together all the dried fruit, chopped lemon, suet, chopped apple, sugar, mixed spices together with the brandy and sherry and mix until thoroughly combined. Cover the bowl with clingfilm and set aside to marinate overnight. The mincemeat can be made weeks before and stored in a cool dark place to mature. If you prefer, the mincemeat filling can be placed into a food processor and pulsed and blended slightly to create a smoother mix, however I love to keep all the ingredients whole.

To make the pastry, blend the flour, baking powder, butter and sugar in a food processor until the mixture resembles fine breadcrumbs. Add the egg yolks and a touch of cold water if required to bring the mixture together to form the pastry. Turn out the dough onto a lightly floured surface and knead lightly, wrap the pastry in clingfilm and chill in the fridge for half an hour. This pastry can easily be made by hand if you do not have a food processor.

Preheat the oven to 180C/350F/Gas mark 4. Lightly grease a shallow 12 hole small yorkshire pudding/cake tin. Remove the pastry from the fridge and roll out on a lightly floured surface to a thickness of 1/4inch. Using a round fluted pastry cutter, cut out discs to fit the holes in the baking tray and place the pastry discs inside the holes. Carefully fill heaped spoonfuls of the mincemeat into the pastry discs. Cut out the remaining pastry into slightly smaller discs to form the tops. Brush the rims of the pastry cases with a little beaten egg and place the lids on. Press the edges lightly together to form a seal.

Brush the tops of the pastry with a little extra beaten egg, using a tip of knife, cut a small stream hole in the lid of each pie and bake in the preheated oven for 20-25 minutes, or until golden brown. Remove the pies from the oven, allow to cool slightly in the tray, then serve still warm dusted with a little icing sugar or with brandy butter.

Gingerbread Men (Makes 15-20 Gingerbread Men)

This recipe can be used for biscuits or pretty Christmas tree decorations.

350g/12oz plain flour
1 tsp ground ginger
1/2 tsp ground cloves
1/2 tsp ground cinnamon
1 tsp bicarbonate of soda
110g/4oz butter
175g/6oz soft brown sugar
1 egg
4 tbsps golden syrup

Method

Sieve together the flour, spices and bicarbonate of soda into a large mixing bowl. Rub in the butter until it resembles fine breadcrumbs, then add the sugar. Add the beaten egg and the golden syrup, then mix together to form a dough. Tip out onto a work surface and knead for a minute until the dough is smooth.

Preheat oven to 180C/350F/Gas mark 4. Roll out the dough to about 5mm thick, then cut out shapes using a biscuit cutter. Lay the biscuits onto a baking sheet lined with baking parchment paper, then bake for 10-15 minutes until golden brown. Remove from the oven, allow to cool slightly on the tray, then carefully transfer to a wire rack to cool completely. Store in an air tight tin.

Tip: If using the biscuits to create tree decorations, punch a hole using a drinking straw prior to cooking, if the hole closes during cooking, re-open the hole when the biscuits are still warm, as they are cooling on the tray. Thread with ribbon to hang on the tree. Decorate the gingerbread men with icing, chocolates or coloured sweets.

Hot Cross Buns (Makes 12)

500g/1lb 2oz strong white bread flour
50g/2oz butter
50g/2oz caster sugar
1 tsp salt
1/2 tsp ground allspice
1 tsp ground cinnamon
1/2 tsp ground nutmeg
1 1/2 tsp dried yeast
1 egg, beaten
280ml/10 fl oz whole milk
110g/4oz raisins
25g/1oz mixed peel

For the cross
110g/4oz strong white flour
130ml/4 1/2 fl oz water

To glaze
2 tbsps caster sugar
4 tbsps whole milk

Method

Place the flour into a large bowl and rub in the butter, then stir in the caster sugar, spices and yeast. Add the beaten egg and the milk and mix well until all the ingredients are thoroughly combined and bring the mixture together to form a soft pliable dough.

Transfer the dough to a lightly floured work surface and knead for 5 minutes until the dough is silky smooth and elastic in texture. Work in the raisins and mixed peel. Return the dough to the bowl, loosely cover with clingfilm and set aside in a warm place to prove for about an hour, or until doubled in size. Tip the dough onto the work surface and knead well to knock the air out, then divide into 12 equal pieces. Dust your hands with some flour and with your hands cupped and fingers open take each piece of dough and rotate your hand in a circular motion, pressing down on the dough to create a neat ball. Repeat with the rest of the dough.

159

Place the buns onto 2 oiled baking trays, lightly cover with clingfilm and once again set aside in a warm draught free place to rise for half an hour. Preheat the oven to 200C/400F/Gas mark 6.

To make the cross, place the flour and water into a bowl and mix well to create a smooth wet paste. Spoon the mixture into a piping bag, snip off the end and carefully pipe a cross on top of the buns. Bake in the preheated oven for 15-20 minutes, or until well risen and golden.

Meanwhile, to make the glaze, place the milk and sugar into a small pan and heat gently to dissolve the sugar. Increase the temperature and boil for 2-3 minutes, stirring occasionally until the mixture is syrupy. Remove the buns from the oven and brush with the glaze. Transfer the buns to a wire rack and leave to cool before serving.

Easter-Nest Cupcakes (20-24 cupcakes)

175g/6oz of flour
75g/2 1/2oz of cocoa powder
175g/6oz of sugar
2 eggs
1 tsp baking soda
110g/4oz of butter (softened)
225ml/8 fl oz of milk
1 tsp vanilla
1/2 tsp salt
For milk chocolate icing topping
350g/12oz milk chocolate (broken into pieces)
6 tbsps butter (softened)
280g/10oz of icing sugar
50ml/2 fl oz of milk
1 tsp vanilla
12 chocolate flake bars
large pack of mini-chocolate eggs

Method

Preheat the oven to 180C/350F/Gas mark 4. Line a cupcake baking tray with paper liners. Place the cocoa powder, flour, baking soda and salt in a bowl and mix together.

Place the sugar, vanilla, eggs and butter in a large bowl and beat together. Add the milk and carefully beat in the flour/cocoa mixture. Spoon the mixture into the cupcake liners, up to about 1/2 full. Place in the oven and bake for 20 minutes. Remove from the oven and leave to cool for 5-10 minutes. Transfer onto a wire cooling rack to cool completely.

To make the icing, place the milk chocolate in a small bowl and add the butter. Place in a pan of hot water and heat over a medium heat, stirring the chocolate until it melts. Transfer the mixture to a large bowl and gradually beat in the icing sugar, alternating it with milk. Finally, stir in the vanilla. Spread generously on each of the cooled cupcakes. Cut each of the chocolate flakes in half and then cut them in half, lengthways. Arrange the pieces of flake around the top of each egg, giving a nest-like appearance (use the icing to stick parts together, if needed). Place 3 mini-eggs in the centre of each arrangement.

My recipes

Recipe ....

Serves ....

Preparation time ....

Notes/tips ....

....

....

....

Ingredients ....

....

....

....

....

....

....

....

....

Method

My recipes

Recipe ....

Serves ....

Preparation time ....

Notes/tips ....

....

....

....

Ingredients ....

....

....

....

....

....

....

Method

My recipes

Recipe ....

Serves ....

Preparation time ....

Notes/tips ....

....

....

....

Ingredients

....

....

....

....

....

....

....

....

Method

My recipes

Recipe ....

Serves ....

Preparation time ....

Notes/tips ....

....

....

....

Ingredients

Method

My recipes

Recipe ....

Serves ....

Preparation time ....

Notes/tips ....

....

....

....

Ingredients

....

....

....

....

....

....

....

Method

My recipes

Recipe ....

Serves ....

Preparation time ....

Notes/tips ....

....

....

....

Ingredients ....

....

....

....

....

....

....

....

Method

List of recipes

Bread

Cakes

Biscuit & Cookies

Spoons to millilitres

1/2 teaspoon	2.5 ml	1 tablespoon	15 ml
1 teaspoon	5 ml	2 tablespoons	30 ml
1 & 1/2 teaspoons	7.5 ml	3 tablespoons	45 ml
2 teaspoons	10 ml	4 tablespoons	60 ml

Grams to ounces

10g	0.25oz	225g	8oz
15g	0.38oz	250g	9oz
25g	1oz	280g	10oz
50g	2oz	325g	11oz
85g	3oz	350g	12oz
110g	4oz	375g	13oz
150g	5oz	400g	14oz
175g	6oz	425g	15oz
200g	7oz	450g	16oz/1lb

Liquid measures

5fl oz	1/4 pint	150 ml
7.5fl oz		215 ml
10fl oz	1/2 pint	280 ml
15fl oz		425 ml
20fl oz	1 pint	570 ml
35fl oz		1 litre

The recipes contained in this book are passed on in good faith but the publisher cannot be held responsible for any adverse results. Please be aware that certain recipes may contain nuts. Spoon measurements are level, teaspoons are assumed to be 5ml, tablespoons 15ml. For other measurements, see chart above. Times given are for guidance only, as preparation techniques may vary and can lead to different cooking times.